I0817203

SPORTS SUPERSTARS

# SIDNEY CROSBY

By Kevin Frederickson

Kaleidoscope
Minneapolis, MN

*Your Front Row Seat to the Games*

This edition is co-published by agreement between
Kaleidoscope and World Book, Inc.

Kaleidoscope Publishing, Inc.
6012 Blue Circle Drive
Minnetonka, MN 55343 U.S.A.

World Book, Inc.
180 North LaSalle St., Suite 900
Chicago IL 60601 U.S.A.



Kaleidoscope ISBNs
978-1-64519-047-9 (library bound)
978-1-64494-204-8 (paperback)
978-1-64519-148-3 (ebook)

World Book ISBN
978-0-7166-4351-7 (library bound)

Library of Congress Control Number
2019940066



Printed in the United States of America.

TABLE OF
# CONTENTS


Chapter 1: Golden Goal .......... 4

Chapter 2: The Next One .......... 10

Chapter 3: Helping Others .......... 16

Chapter 4: Ups and Downs .......... 22

Beyond the Book .......... 28

Research Ninja .......... 29

Further Resources .......... 30

Glossary .......... 31

Index .......... 32

Photo Credits .......... 32

About the Author .......... 32

CHAPTER 1

# Golden Goal

Sidney Crosby charges toward the net. But two US defensemen get in his way. The goalie blocks a soft shot into the corner. Crosby again charges after it. He collects the puck. But defenseman Brian Rafalski is chasing after him. A referee gets in the way, too. Crosby almost loses the puck. But at the last moment, he flails his stick. The puck gets to teammate Jarome Iginla in the corner. And the biggest moment in Crosby's career is underway.

*All of Canada looked to Sidney Crosby going into the 2010 Olympics in Vancouver.*

*Team Canada fell to Team USA 5–3 earlier in the 2010 Olympic tournament.*

It's the 2010 Olympic Winter Games. Crosby and Team Canada are going for the gold medal. Olympic hockey is always a big deal in Canada. But this year is bigger than most. That's because the game is in Vancouver, British Columbia. And heating things up further, Canada is facing its **rival**, Team USA.

Nearly 18,000 fans are in the arena. Millions more watch on TV. Canada fans are getting antsy, though. Their team once led 2–0. Now they're tied 2–2. And the game is more than seven minutes into overtime. A goal would clinch the gold medal. Both teams need a hero to step up.

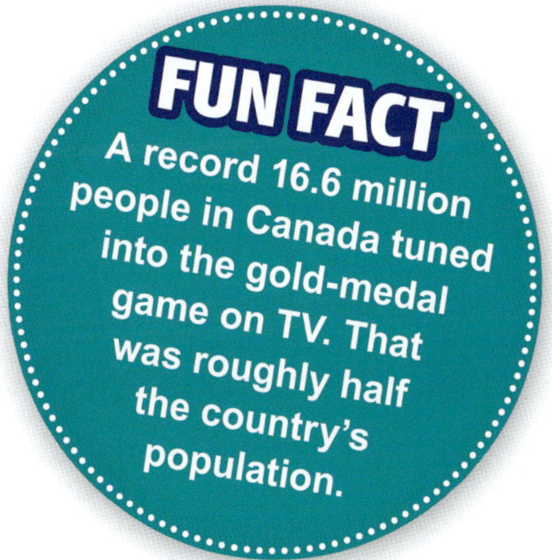

Crosby, left, celebrates his gold-medal-winning goal at the 2010 Olympics.

"Iggy!"

Suddenly, Crosby sees a gap. He takes off toward the goal. Iginla hears him calling. He knows just where Crosby will be. But Iginla starts falling to the ice. He swings his stick. It's a perfect pass.

Crosby collects it on the backhand. He effortlessly moves the puck to his forehand. Then he releases a wrist shot.

Goal!

"Sid the Kid" has done it. Canada is the Olympic champion!

Crosby raises his arms. Teammates rush over to celebrate. Fans across the country celebrate, too. They have cheered for Crosby since he was a teenager. Now he is twenty-two. And he has just scored one of the biggest goals in Canada's hockey history.

## LEADING TO GOLD

**Crosby returned to Team Canada for the 2014 Olympics. This time, Crosby was team captain. The Olympics were in Russia. Canada won its first five games. Then it faced Sweden for the gold medal. Canada won 3–0. Crosby scored one of the goals. He left with another gold medal.**

CHAPTER 2

# The Next One

Sidney Crosby fires a shot. It goes into the net. Sidney fires another shot. It misses the net. Bam! The puck slams against a dryer. That's because Sidney is in his basement. He spends many hours there. He takes shot after shot.

*Sidney's old dryer was put on display at the Nova Scotia Sport Hall of Fame.*

Many go into the net. But many others hit the dryer. They often leave dents. But Sidney never stops practicing.

Sidney Crosby was born on August 7, 1987. He grew up in Cole Harbour, Nova Scotia. Hockey is a popular sport there. Sidney started shooting pucks with his dad at two years old. By the time Sidney was three, he was out on the ice skating.

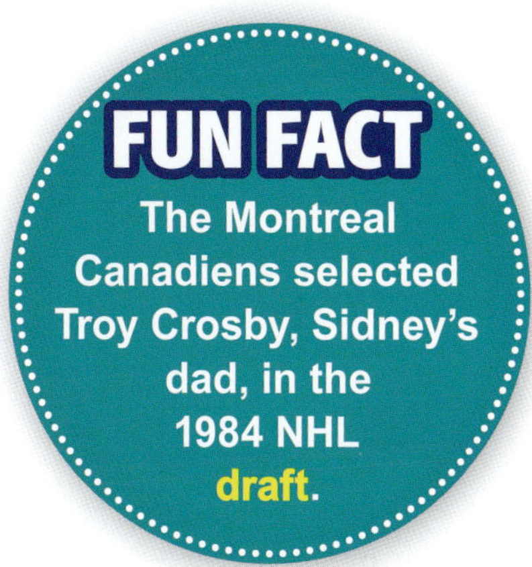

Growing up, Sidney, right, was often compared to the legendary Wayne Gretzky, left.

**FUN FACT**

**In 2002, hockey magazine *The Hockey News* called Sidney "The Next One." This was a play on Wayne Gretzky's nickname "The Great One."**

Sidney loved hockey. Often he was on the rink with his friends. If not, he could usually be found shooting pucks in his basement. Sidney also tried to learn from the best. He watched a lot of videos. He studied how greats such as Wayne Gretzky played.

Before long, Sidney's talent was obvious. At age six, he signed up for a team. The team was for ten-year-olds. The other players were bigger than Sidney. But he was very skilled. This helped him keep up.

Sidney continued playing against older kids. When he was fourteen, he played in the Air Canada Cup. Most of the players were sixteen or seventeen. It hardly mattered. Sidney was the leading scorer. He was also named Most Valuable Player (MVP).

**Scouts** began to take notice. So did other players. Some were jealous of Sidney. They bullied him on the ice. Sidney decided to make a change.

In 2005, Sidney led his junior team Rimouski Océanic on a 35-game undefeated streak.

In 2002, Sidney moved to Faribault, Minnesota. He played for Shattuck-St. Mary's School. It is known for its great hockey team.

Sidney was soon ready for another challenge. The next year he joined a **junior** team in Canada. These junior leagues are competitive. Many future pros play in them. But Sidney was still a star. He played 59 games for Rimouski Océanic in 2003–04. He scored an amazing 135 **points**. The next year he had 168 points in 62 games. He also led his team to the championship. It was clear he was ready for the next level.

# Where Crosby Has Been

**1** **Cole Harbour, Nova Scotia:** Sidney Crosby was born here on August 7, 1987.

**2** **Bathurst, New Brunswick:** Crosby starred at the 2002 Air Canada Cup as a youth hockey player.

**3** **Faribault, Minnesota:** Crosby played one year at Shattuck-St. Mary's School.

**4** **Rimouski, Quebec:** Crosby played two seasons of junior hockey for Rimouski Océanic.

**5** **Pittsburgh, Pennsylvania:** Crosby has played for the Penguins since they drafted him first overall in 2005.

**6** **Detroit, Michigan:** Crosby won his first Stanley Cup championship in 2009 when the Penguins defeated the Detroit Red Wings in seven games.

**7** **Vancouver, British Columbia:** Crosby scored the winning goal in overtime as Canada won the 2010 Olympic gold medal.

**8** **San Jose, California:** In 2016, Crosby won his second Stanley Cup when the Penguins defeated the Sharks.

CHAPTER 3

# Helping Others

"Hi, Sidney Crosby."

The Pittsburgh Penguins star looked back. A young boy skated by. The boy wore a Crosby jersey. Now he wanted to talk to the star.

Crosby and his teammates were leading a hockey camp. Many kids were starstruck. They were too nervous to approach the players. But not this kid.

"I saw you on TV," he said.

Crosby was surprised. The game was late at night. But he was eager to hear more. He bent low to speak to the young fan. They talked some more. Then the youngster skated off.

Crosby is passionate about hockey. He works with the Penguins to lead camps for local kids.

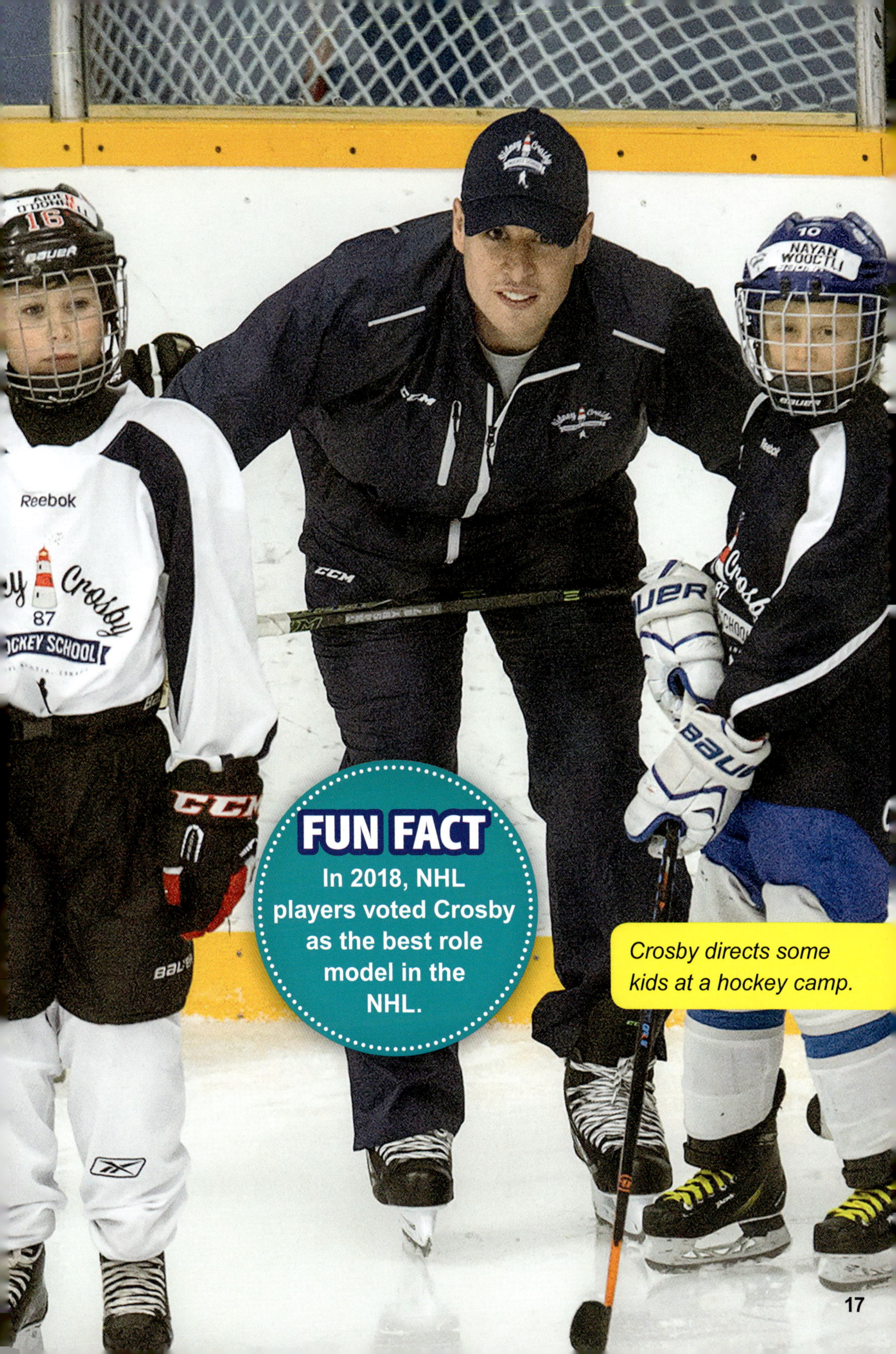


## FUN FACT

In 2018, NHL players voted Crosby as the best role model in the NHL.

*Crosby directs some kids at a hockey camp.*

**FUN FACT**
Crosby had the highest-selling jersey in the NHL from September 2005 to February 2008.

*Crosby quickly became one of the NHL's most popular players.*

Crosby races toward the net. He spins. His back is to the net. Then he shoots the puck between his legs. This isn't an NHL game, though. It's not even a game. Crosby is in an advertisement. He is showing off his skills.

Crosby is a huge star. Fans knew of him even before he reached the NHL. Many companies have taken notice. They pay Crosby to **endorse** their products. In 2017–18, Crosby earned $4.8 million from such deals. No NHL player earned more.

# CAREER STATS

Through the 2018–19 season

| | |
|---|---|
| GAMES PLAYED | 943 |
| ASSISTS | 770 |
| GOALS | 446 |
| STANLEY CUP CHAMPIONSHIPS | 3 |

*Crosby shows off the Stanley Cup in a parade in Dartmouth, Nova Scotia, in 2017.*

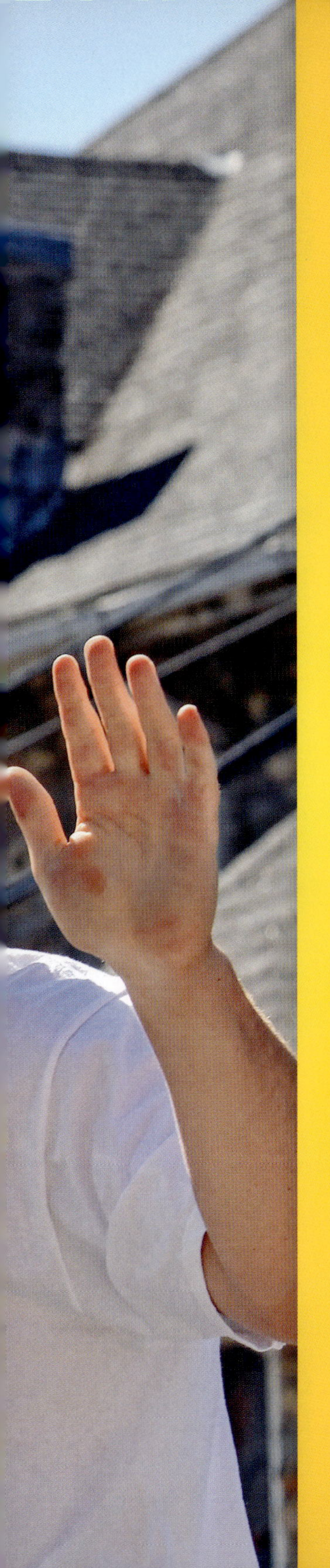

Crosby doesn't like to talk about his personal life. He doesn't use social media much. But he likes spending time with his family. He also likes giving back to his hometown.

Crosby left Cole Harbour as a teenager. But he still does lots of **charity** work there. In 2011, he donated 87 sets of new hockey equipment. He also has hosted the Sidney Crosby Hockey School. Kids from across Nova Scotia attended. Crosby helped them improve their hockey skills.

Crosby also goes home for special events. In 2017, he won his third Stanley Cup. For the third time, he brought it home. The city again held a parade. Crosby also brought the trophy to hospitals so sick fans could see it.

CHAPTER 4

Crosby celebrates scoring his first NHL goal in an October 2005 game against the Boston Bruins.

# Ups and Downs

Sidney Crosby shot the puck. Then he raced in to get the **rebound**. Two Pittsburgh Penguins teammates whiffed. So Crosby collected the puck. Then he shot it. The puck went right into the goal.

"Yeah!" he shouted. Teammates rushed to Crosby. Only 18 years old, he had just scored his first NHL goal.

**FUN FACT**
When Crosby joined the NHL, he lived with Penguins superstar Mario Lemieux. It was Lemieux's final season.

And it came in only his third NHL game. He had already recorded four **assists**.

The Penguins had picked him first in the 2005 NHL Draft. Fans had high expectations. Crosby quickly lived up to them. He scored 102 points as a **rookie** in 2005–06. One year later he had 120. No one in the NHL had more.

Time was running out. The Penguins charged into the Detroit Red Wings' zone. Crosby got the puck. He sent it toward the goal. It just barely went wide. Just like that, the game was over. Detroit had won the 2008 Stanley Cup.

One year later the teams met again. The Stanley Cup Final was close. But this time the Penguins won. Two men carried the Cup onto the ice. Crosby skated to center ice. He posed for a photo. Then he raised the Cup high above his head and screamed. Crosby was just twenty-one. That made him the youngest captain to lead a team to the Cup.

## RIVALS FROM THE START

**Alexander Ovechkin was the top pick in the 2004 NHL Draft. Crosby was the top pick in 2005. But the NHL cancelled the 2004–05 season. That meant both started in 2005–06. Both players quickly became stars. Ovechkin was known as a great scorer. Crosby played a more balanced game. Their teams, the Penguins and Washington Capitals, became fierce rivals.**

# CAREER TIMELINE

1987

*August 7, 1987*
Sidney Crosby is born in Cole Harbour, Nova Scotia.

2002

*April 27, 2002*
Crosby and his 16-and-under hockey team reach the Air Canada Cup championship.

2003

*2003*
Rimouski Océanic selects Crosby first in the 2003 Quebec Major Junior Hockey League draft.

2005

*July 30, 2005*
The Pittsburgh Penguins take Crosby with the No. 1 pick in the NHL Draft.

*October 5, 2005*
Crosby gets an assist in his NHL debut with the Penguins.

2009

*June 12, 2009*
Crosby wins his first Stanley Cup as Pittsburgh defeats Detroit in the Final.

2010

*February 28, 2010*
Canada wins the Olympic gold medal as Crosby scores the game-winning goal in overtime.

2014

*February 23, 2014*
Crosby leads Team Canada to another Olympic gold medal in Sochi, Russia.

2017

*June 11, 2017*
Crosby helps the Penguins to their second straight Stanley Cup championship.

Crosby took a hard hit in 2011. Soon after he took another one. He began to feel dizzy. He got headaches. At times, he felt he might throw up. He had gotten a **concussion**. And he wasn't feeling better. Crosby missed game after game. He wondered if he'd ever play again. In total he missed big parts of two seasons.

Finally, he began to feel better. He played most of the 2013–14 season. And he quickly returned to form. Crosby led a re-tooled Penguins team. In 2016, they won a Stanley Cup. One year later they won again. There was no doubt. Crosby was one of the greatest players ever.

*Crosby reached the 100-point mark for the sixth time in 2018–19.*

# BEYOND THE BOOK

**After reading the book, it's time to think about what you learned. Try the following exercises to jumpstart your ideas.**

## THINK

**THAT'S NEWS TO ME.** Crosby won his first Stanley Cup in 2009. How might news sources be able to fill in more details about this? What new information could you find in news articles? Where could you go to find those sources?

## CREATE

**PRIMARY SOURCES.** A primary source is a firsthand account. Make a list of different primary sources you might be able to find about the 2010 Olympics. What new information might you learn from these sources?

## SHARE

**SUM IT UP.** Write one paragraph summarizing the important points from this book. Make sure it's in your own words. Don't just copy what is in the text. Share the paragraph with a classmate. What questions does your classmate have about the summary? What additional questions does he or she have about Crosby?

## GROW

**REAL-LIFE RESEARCH.** What places could you visit to learn more about Crosby? What other things could you learn while you were there?

Visit www.ninjaresearcher.com/0479 to learn how to take your research skills and book report writing to the next level!

**SEARCH LIKE A PRO**
Learn about how to use search engines to find useful websites.

**FACT OR FAKE?**
Discover how you can tell a trusted website from an untrustworthy resource.

**TEXT DETECTIVE**
Explore how to zero in on the information you need most.

**SHOW YOUR WORK**
Research responsibly—learn how to cite sources.

## WRITE

**GET TO THE POINT**
Learn how to express your main ideas.

**PLAN OF ATTACK**
Learn prewriting exercises and create an outline.

DOWNLOADABLE REPORT FORMS

# Further Resources

## BOOKS

Fishman, Jon M. *Hockey's G.O.A.T.: Wayne Gretzky, Sidney Crosby, and More*. Lerner Publications, 2020.

Hall, Brian. *Sidney Crosby: Hockey Star*. North Star Editions, 2018.

Rauf, Don. *Sidney Crosby.* Rosen Central, 2019.

## WEBSITES

Factsurfer.com gives you a safe, fun way to find more information.

1. Go to www.factsurfer.com.
2. Enter "Sidney Crosby" into the search box and click 🔍.
3. Select your book cover to see a list of related websites.

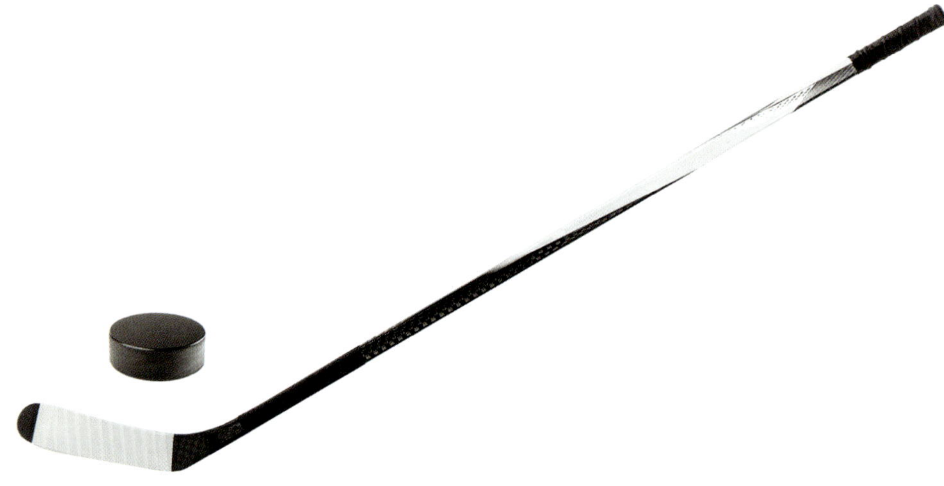

# Glossary

**assist:** An assist is a pass or deflection that leads to a goal; in hockey each goal can have as many as two assists. Crosby got the assist on his teammate's goal.

**charity:** Charity is work in which one gives back to others. Crosby is involved in charity work around Pittsburgh.

**concussion:** A concussion is a brain injury caused by contact to the head. Crosby suffered a concussion after being hit in the head during a game.

**draft:** A draft is a system leagues use to add new talent to their teams. Crosby was the first pick in the 2005 NHL Draft.

**endorse:** To endorse means to support something in return for pay. Many companies pay Crosby to endorse their products.

**junior:** Junior hockey is for players ages sixteen through twenty. Crosby was one of the top junior players in all of Canada.

**rebound:** A rebound is when a goalie makes a save but the puck goes back into play. Crosby shot and then scored on a rebound.

**rival:** A rival is an opponent with whom a player or team has an intense history. Canada and the United States are big rivals in hockey.

**rookie:** A rookie is a player in his first season in a league. Crosby scored 102 points as a rookie.

**scout:** A scout is a person who watches and develops opinions on different players. Many scouts thought Crosby would be a great NHL player.

# Index

Cole Harbour, Nova Scotia, 11, 15, 21, 25
concussion, 26
Crosby, Troy, 11

Detroit Red Wings, 15, 24
dryer, 10–11

Gretzky, Wayne, 12, 13

Iginla, Jarome, 4, 8

Lemieux, Mario, 23

Montreal Canadiens, 11

NHL Draft, 11, 15, 23, 24, 25

Olympic Games, 7–9, 15, 25
Ovechkin, Alexander, 24

Pittsburgh Penguins, 15, 16, 22–24, 25, 26

Rafalski, Brian, 4
Rimouski Océanic, 14, 15, 25

Shattuck-St. Mary's School, 14, 15
Sidney Crosby Hockey School, 21
Stanley Cup, 15, 19, 21, 24, 25, 26

Washington Capitals, 24

## PHOTO CREDITS

The images in this book are reproduced through the courtesy of: David Kirouac/Icon Sportswire/AP Images, front cover (center); Jeanine Leech/Icon Sportswire/AP Images, front cover (right), p. 3; Eugene Onischenko/Shutterstock Images, front cover (background); Sergei Bachlakov/Shutterstock Images, p. 4; Matt Slocum/AP Images, pp. 4–5; Gene J. Puskar/AP Images, pp. 6–7, 19 (Sidney Crosby), 22–23, 26–27; Chris O'Meara/AP Images, p. 8; Andrew Vaughan/The Canadian Press/AP Images, pp. 10, 12–13, 16–17; Paul McKinnon/Shutterstock Images, pp. 11, 20–21, 21; David Duprey/AP Images, p. 14; Red Line Editorial, pp. 15, 19 (chart), 25 (timeline); Jai Agnish/Shutterstock Images, pp. 18, 24; Longchalerm Rungruang/Shutterstock Images, pp. 25 (top), 30 (hockey stick); aperturesound/Shutterstock Images, pp. 25 (bottom), 30 (puck); Mark Humphrey/AP Images, p. 26.

## ABOUT THE AUTHOR

Kevin Frederickson is a freelance writer and editor from Ohio. He lives near Cincinnati with his golden doodle, Max.